Beginners Guide to
Blockchain Technology

Table of Contents

Introduction

The internet is absolutely filled these days with the buzz of blockchains and how they are changing the world. From the humble beginnings of Satoshi Nakamoto's iconic white paper on bitcoin to the enormous market capitalization and capital raising figures posted by cryptocurrencies and ICOs (Initial Coin Offerings) this year 2017 alone, one thing is clear – blockchain technology is here to stay!

No longer is the technology the exclusive preserve of computer hobbyists and digital currency enthusiasts as more and more industries are finding new and intuitive ways to take advantage of the technology. Entrepreneurs, Organizations and even Government agencies are making significant inroads into expanding the applicability of blockchain technology.

With all of these developments happening ever so quickly, it is important to gain the necessary background knowledge on the basics of the technology. While it involves a great deal of technical knowledge, it is indeed possible for even a complete computer neophyte to get a firm understanding of the concepts and features of blockchains.

The book is written in a manner that is simple to understand. Technical concepts have been fleshed out and explained in such a way as not to be confusing for beginners.

Chapter 1
Introduction to Blockchains

These days, the internet is seemingly saturated with several examples of blockchains. No matter where you turn on the social web, there are posts dedicated to different cryptocurrencies, ICOs (Initial Coin Offerings), and blockchain-based applications, just to mention a few. Blockchain technology is arguably one of the most popular emerging technologies in the world today. It has single-handedly ushered the world into another phase of computer technology that has resulted in sweeping changes across many spheres of human endeavor. Individuals, Entrepreneurs, Corporations and even Governments are investing time, effort and resources into developing more intuitive blockchain applications to provide solutions for diverse problems.

Definition

Ever wondered why it is called a "blockchain"? Well, blockchains literally owe their names to the way in which data is stored in blocks linked together by chains. Blockchains are an extensive database of transactions that are grouped together into transaction blocks when then link together in a linear sequence to form the blockchain. The entire blockchain resides in a network which is governed by certain rules embedded in the system.

A blockchain can be defined as a shared distributed ledger that contains the record of transactions between participants in a

3

decentralized network. Every participating node in a blockchain network has access to the shared ledger and can initiate and/or authenticate transactions on the blockchain. Every transaction is validated by means of a consensus agreement within the decentralized network. This sounds a bit technical, so let's break it down a bit.

1. It is a shared distributed ledger. For those unfamiliar with a ledger, it is a record of transactions, much like a simple credit statement. Instead of having multiple ledgers for the participants of a network, a blockchain has only one ledger that is distributed throughout the entire network. This is known generally as the Distributed Ledger Technology (DLT). The blockchain is regarded as the first successful implementation of the DLT framework. This concept will be discussed in more detail in the "History of the Blockchain" section of this chapter.

2. Every participating node in the network has a copy of the ledger. This is to ensure transparency and decentralization. Most computer systems are centralized, meaning that there is a central server that controls the operation of the system and maintains the network. Think of your school, office or even your email client. Your computer is connected to a central network that is responsible for administering the network. Because blockchains are decentralized, there is no central server and information flow is between network peers.

3. Blockchains rely on a majority consensus in order to maintain order within the network. With no hierarchy in a decentralized network, there must be a way to agree on certain parameters within the network. This agreement is reached by a majority of the nodes coming to a mutual consensus on said parameters.

Blockchain Fundamentals

- Distributed Ledger Technology (DLT)

  A blockchain is basically a group of computing nodes forming a network in which transactions are carried out without the need for a central authority to validate the transactions. Because there are transactions involved, there needs to be a record of these transactions and with the absence of a central authority in the network, the task of maintaining this transaction record falls on every member of the network.

  This is the basic principle of operation of the DLT framework. So for example, if 100 computing nodes form a blockchain network, and some of these nodes are department stores, students, doctors and so on, instead of each node having a separate ledger where they record their individual transactions, the entire network has one ledger. This singular ledger is then shared throughout the network with regular updates being made once a transaction is validated.

- Permissions

In terms of permission, blockchains can either be public or private. Public blockchains are permissionless while private blockchains are permissioned. Permissionless blockchains do have any constraint imposed on a user's ability to participate in the network. All that is required to become a connected node in the network is to download the blockchain client (like Bitcoin, Ethereum etc.) and connect with neighboring nodes (peers). For the permissioned network, special access has to be granted before a user can become a node on the network.

Government agencies and Corporations usually make use of permissioned blockchains due to the sensitive nature of the transactions that are carried out within such networks. Most of the well-known blockchains and cryptocurrencies in the world today like Bitcoin, Ethereum and Nxt use public (permissionless) blockchains. The need for permissioned blockchains arises from the desire to enforce data protection regulations and that is why it is most favored by Government agencies and large Corporations. Another reason for the adoption of permissioned blockchains is based on the need to regulate the consistency of the data that is added to the blockchain database.

In permissioned blockchains, there are also protocols in place that can restrict the information that can be viewed by certain nodes. This is similar to what obtains in the Intelligence community where only people at certain security clearance levels can have access to particular information. For the purpose of this book, all focus will be restricted to permissionless (public) blockchains.

- Majority Consensus

As stated earlier in this book, there is no central authority in a blockchain network. In other to achieve network-wide homogeneity of the blockchain, a mechanism of achieving majority consensus has to be established within the operating protocols of the blockchain network. What this means is that when creating a blockchain, the developers have to create a method that will allow a majority of the participating nodes to vote on what they believe should be the true state of affairs of the blockchain.

The most common cause of conflict in a blockchain is in the validation of transactions. An intuitive method of coming to consensus is necessary to maintain the fidelity of a blockchain network. Since there is no central authority to enforce homogeneity, complex mathematical computations are used instead to make sure that everyone is following the same rules. There are several iterations of these complex mathematical computations such as Proof of Work (PoW), Proof of Stake (PoS), Proof of Burn (PoB), Multisig (Multi-Signature), and Practical Byzantine Fault Tolerance (PBFT) among others. Many of these mathematical algorithms will be explained in subsequent chapters of this book.

History of Blockchains

Part 1: Primitive Cryptography

The history of blockchains is a collection of the history of the base technologies on which the blockchain is built upon which are the distributed ledger, P2P network, and cryptography (or more specifically, public key cryptography). This is by no means the complete list of all the constituent technical aspects of a blockchain but for the purpose of this book, these 3 will suffice. Of these 3 core technologies, the one that ties in most profoundly with the history of the blockchain is cryptography. In many ways, it is accurate to say that blockchains are the manifestation of one of the advancements in cryptographic technology – public key cryptography.

There are many history experts who posit that cryptography is almost as old as man. Due to the lack of information and the abundance of mystery surrounding the activities of man during those early epochs, it can be decidedly difficult to ascertain whether the departure from the norm in terms of how written records were kept in the form of hieroglyphs or cuneiform on the tombs of certain individuals was cryptic or perhaps just ceremonial. There are however texts that survive from early Indian civilizations that point to the use of codes and secret messages in conveying information to spies.

The first recognized form of encryption was the "substitution cipher" which shows up in many different civilizations such as Hebrew, Indian, Egyptian, and even Greek civilizations from between 500 BCE to 200 CE. Many of these substitution ciphers were monoalphabetic. Apart from substitution ciphers, some civilizations like the Spartans favored the transposition cipher. These cryptographic systems carried on even up till the time of Julius Caesar who was known to use a 3 shift substitution cipher where the key was three alphabets after the encrypted code. So if the letter in the code was A, the key would be D and so on and so forth until the code was deciphered.

It is important to understand that as cryptography developed, so did the counterpart decryption technology also develop. These early forms of cryptography depended solely on the inherent secrecy of the system. This meant that if the encryption system was known, the code became useless. During the Middle Ages and towards the start of the modern era, there was a shift in focus from keeping the secrecy of the encryption system, to ensure the secrecy of the encryption key. This singular shift in focus led to the rise of more sophisticated encryption technology.

Part 2: Two World Wars, Enigma, and the AES

World War 1 saw the invention of the Enigma machine which would remain the pinnacle of encryption technology until it was decrypted during World War 2. In the wake of the rapid industrialization and the assimilation of military technocrats into the private sector after World War 2, cryptographic technology began to migrate from the military scene to the business scene with many Corporations like IBM beginning to see the potential for secure business transactions powered by robust encryption systems. This led to the development of the Data Encryption Standard (DES) which remained the mainstream encryption standard from 1973 to 1997 when it was finally decrypted using brute force computing.

Part 3: DES and Cryptographic Keys

By the year 2000, the Advanced Encryption Standard (AES) was created but was still susceptible to brute force attack. These days, the standard for cryptography is the Cryptographic Key which is a marked departure from every other form of cryptography known to man. From the basic substitution ciphers to the DES, encryption was dependent on symmetric key algorithms. Because the keys are symmetric, they could be easily hacked as the code for the key was known to both sender and receiver. In Cryptographic Key protocols, asymmetric keys are used and in so doing, the full code to decrypt the cipher is never contained in any one key. Decryption will require for the public key of the sender and receiver to match which makes unauthorized decryption mathematically impossible. There is a more detailed explanation of Cryptographic Keys in Chapter 2 of this book.

Part 4: Early Days of the Blockchain

For all intents and purposes, the blockchain was born in 2008 when the enigmatic Satoshi Nakamoto released the Bitcoin White

Paper. The main highlight of this white paper was the solution to the "double-spend" problem that had plagued the virtual currency scene since its inception. Satoshi Nakamoto introduced a system that combined cryptographic technology, game theory, and computer science within the framework of a distributed database (DLT) to create a means by which to ensure a means for payment processing.

The Bitcoin Blockchain was the first successful implementation of a framework that removed the need for third-party authentication services. The following year, the Bitcoin Blockchain was released and it has gone on to become the most successful blockchain and cryptocurrency to date.

Part 5: Building on the Bitcoin Blockchain

Seeing the massive success of the Bitcoin Blockchain, many developers began to copy the bitcoin protocol to develop blockchain solutions. Most of these early blockchains were more or less like bitcoin but they were not as successful as bitcoin. In the years immediately following 2009, the blockchain scene became saturated with these bitcoin derivatives. However, as time went on and scalability became an issue, some developers saw the need to improve upon the bitcoin protocol, focusing their attention on not just the payment processing ability of bitcoin but the immense potentials inherent in blockchain technology.

Part 6: The Ethereum Blockchain

In 2014, Vitalik Buterin released Ethereum which was in many ways, a massive improvement to the standards set by bitcoin. Ethereum was more than just a payment processing blockchain; it was a total blockchain protocol that allowed other developers to build blockchain-based applications on top of it. It also introduced smart contracts to the blockchain scene which has immense potential for being applicable in many spheres of human endeavor. Some have even gone to calling Ethereum the embodiment of the Internet of Things.

Part 7: Conclusion

The blockchain is less than a decade old and already, a lot has been achieved, from improved payment processing protocols to a robust smart contracting framework. The future looks bright for the industry as more intuitive blockchain-based solutions are being introduced almost on a daily basis.

Chapter 2
How the Blockchain Technology Works.

Blockchain technology is undoubtedly one of the most popular emerging technologies in the world today. While the concept might seem novel to some, the truth is that it is a combination of some well-known technological advancements. What makes blockchains unique is the way in which these principal technologies are made to function seamlessly with one another. This robust functioning framework is what gives blockchains their appeal and enable them to find almost limitless applicability. These principal technologies upon which the blockchain is built are three in number and they are:

1. Cryptographic Keys.

2. P2P Networks

3. Network Servicing Protocol

In order to gain some level of understanding of the blockchain technology as a whole, these basics of these three principal technologies as well as how they function in the blockchain must be understood.

Cryptographic Keys:

Since time immemorial, the essence of encryption and cryptographic technology was to provide security. There has always been a need to ensure the fidelity of information when it is being transferred from one point to another. The emergence of the Internet and the associated massive advancements in information technology has made data encryption to be of paramount importance. With communication happening on a per second basis between millions of nodes on the global information highway, there has arisen the need to ensure the fidelity of data streams. Remember that advancements in a positive light often always encourage the development of not so savory technology designed to undermine it. In this case, reference is being made to hacking, identity thefts and other forms of data manipulation.

The field of cryptography and data encryption and cryptography has grown in leaps and bounds over the last few centuries with the development of advanced cryptographic methods. The gold standard today in the world of cryptography and data encryption technology is the Cryptographic Key protocol. A cryptographic key is a data string that is used by a cryptographic algorithm to *"decrypt"* (unlock) a cipher text and display it as plain text or to *"encrypt"* (lock) a plain text and display it as a cipher text. The function of the key depends on what end of the information transfer spectrum it is being used in, i.e. sender or receiver. The sender wishes for the information to remain encrypted and for only the receiver to be able to decrypt it. Think of these keys like regular keys that work in pairs, the sender one has and the receiver has another one. Regular keys can lock or unlock a door, for example, and only the holders of these keys can carry out the locking and unlocking process.

Now that we have a basic understanding of Cryptographic Keys, let us examine how they work in a blockchain environment. Remember that in a blockchain, there is no central authenticating body, no central server, just a network of nodes with no hierarchy. This, therefore, creates a situation where each transacting node is responsible for securing their digital identities. This is achieved by means of a digital signature. A digital signature is a combination of a public key and a private key. Think of this signature like a normal signature, unique to each individual, in this case, each computing node in the blockchain network. When a transaction is to be carried out, these two keys are used to encrypt and decrypt the data file containing the transaction details. The combination of public key and private key cryptography creates a digital identity that makes control over proof of ownership easier to accomplish in a decentralized blockchain network.

However, control over proof of ownership isn't enough to create a secure digital framework. Alone, Cryptographic Keys make it easy to secure and authenticate digital identities. It does not, however, offer up a framework for validating the transactions carried out by these authenticated digital identities. The function of central servers in a centralized network is both authenticating identities and authorizing transactions. It, therefore, means that an additional network framework is required to make the blockchains run efficiently and this brings us to the second principal technology; P2P Networks.

P2P Networks:

Blockchains utilize a decentralized computing network, as against a centralized network that is in use in most of the mainstream Internet. This decentralized (or distributed network) is made of up of many computing nodes and there is no hierarchy in the system, i.e. all nodes are essentially equal. Each node is essentially a peer of another node, hence the name Peer-to-Peer (P2P) network. All known blockchains, both public and private make use of P2P networks with the only difference being in the permission granted to the nodes in the network. This use of P2P networks enable blockchains, especially the public ones to grow exponentially, thus making it easy for new nodes to join the network. It also enhances the anonymity of the participants in the network.

In the early days in the development of the P2P network architecture, all nodes basically carried out the same functions. This meant that a portion of the resources of each node was made available for other nodes to use without any central server in charge of coordinating the activities. These days, P2P networks have evolved from this model to one in which the peers do not necessarily have to carry out the same functions. This has enabled the creation of versatile multifunctional P2P networks capable of finding applications in diverse areas of human interests. This singular advancement in the P2P network has expanded the applicability of P2P networks from the basic Home/Corporate networks and file sharing platforms of the past to more robust networks that can handle advanced functions like the ones carried out in a blockchain network.

The blockchain can be thought of as being a modification of the Internet, or the Internet as it was originally conceived. There are many computing nodes spread across the globe that make up the complete Internet architecture and these nodes do not all carry out the same function. Collaborative P2P networks that have nodes with diverse functions and capabilities make it possible to form blockchains where each node or group of nodes can bring in diverse unique capabilities and resources to improve the robust functionality of the blockchain network. More advanced tasks such as the validation of transactions can, therefore, be carried out by these nodes in the blockchain network.

In a blockchain, there are different types of nodes that carry out various functions all of which contribute to the overall servicing and maintenance of the network without the need for a central server. By being built on a P2P network, blockchains can achieve trustless validation of transactions by means of nodes dedicated to validating the transactions initiated by nodes within the network. In chapter 3 of this book, the different types of nodes in a typical blockchain network will be examined.

Network Servicing Protocol:

The Cryptographic Keys and P2P Networks provide the framework for nodes in the blockchain network to authenticate and validate transactions. With cryptographic keys, users can exchange value on the blockchain, while the P2P network makes it easier to validate the ability of these users to exchange value and of this without the need for a central server. The next question is how do you create an incentive for the maintenance of the network.

It is all well and good to have people contributing computing power to form a network, but how do you introduce and economic value to this shared network. Remember that these computing nodes run on electricity which means that resources are being spent just by participating in the network. Unless you are a computer hobbyist, you might not see the need in joining a blockchain and even if you did, you might not want to contribute to its functioning, especially in carrying out the validation of transactions if there is no reward for such activity. The reason for this is simple, as these blockchains increase in size, the amount of computing power needed to validate transactions increases exponentially and this means more consumption of electricity.

Blockchains solve this problem by introducing a reward-based system for computing nodes that offer their computing power in servicing the network by acting as transaction validators. This is called mining on most blockchains and it is what creates transaction blocks which are added to the blockchain periodically.

Features of a Blockchain

Blockchain technology allows for the creation of customized protocols that can be programmed to carry out any function. This means that while many blockchain types are based upon the core blockchain technology, there are numerous differences that exist between them. These differences express themselves in areas such as the transaction validation technique, maximum transaction block size, and time-lag in verifying transactions just to mention a few. There are, however, some features that are common to all blockchains. These are the key features that without which a network protocol cannot be called a blockchain. These features that are common to all blockchain are as follows:

1. Blockchain Immutability

The distributed ledger that is shared among the participants of the blockchain network is theoretically immutable. Simply put, this means the transaction records in the blockchain cannot be altered once they have been validated and added to the blockchain. The reason for this is simple; the distributed ledger is always in a state of perpetual forward momentum, with transactions being periodically validated and added to the blockchain with the subsequent updates to the ledger for every transaction block added.

Anyone wishing to alter the ledger would have to move faster than the entire blockchain and this is theoretically impossible as the blockchain is supported by the immense hashing power of the constituent computing nodes. Even with a 51% control of the hashing power in a blockchain, there is still a limit to the extent to which past records can be altered. The further down the blockchain you go, the expensive and complex the process needed to alter those transactions become.

In a centralized system, the ledger is held by a central server and all that is required to alter data is to attack the central server. In a blockchain, there is no central server and thus, no single point of entry for malicious attacks that aim to compromise the fidelity of the ledger. Any change in the ledger of a blockchain requires a majority consensus among the nodes in the blockchain. There have been cases where the participants in a blockchain have been unable to come to a consensus about alterations made to the blockchain which then resulted in hard forks. The case of the Ethereum hard fork that led to the creation of two distinct Ethereum blockchains comes to mind.

As the size of the blockchain network expands, its immutability becomes more enhanced. Even in the case of the Ethereum hard fork, the old transactions are still the same in both blockchains. Not even a hard fork could alter the old transactions. This immutability of the blockchain gives it the ability to provide a framework for the provenance of assets. This means that the complete history of an asset on the blockchain can be known at any time.

2. Customized Protocols

Blockchains by design, create a framework whereby programmable protocols can be inserted into the blockchain architecture. While there is a basic core function for every blockchain, developers who understand the source code can write programs/applications that can be built on top of the core function to expand the functionality of the blockchain. These programmable protocols range from simple "if functions" to more complex programs called "smart contracts".

The ability to insert these programmable protocols enhances the automation of the blockchain architecture. This, in turn, creates benefits like faster transaction speeds, the creation of an intuitive blockchain-based application, and increased applicability of the blockchain among others. While you may think the Ethereum blockchain was the first blockchain to introduce the smart contract protocol, the truth is that Bitcoin has the ability to create smart contracts. The only difference is that a lot of protocol application layering is required to create smart contracts on the Bitcoin blockchain, whereas in the Ethereum blockchain, this capability is embedded directly into the core blockchain architecture.

3. Transaction Linkage

In all blockchains, every transaction record is linked to a previous transaction along the chain. This is what gives blockchain their names as they are quite literally blocks of transactions linked one to another along a chain all the way up to the first transaction in the chain. This first transaction is called the "Genesis Block". Any node running the full client of the blockchain can examine all the transaction blocks if they so wish to do so. It is possible to retrace and reconstruct the full history of every transaction block and the assets used in the transaction.

The progression common to most blockchains is a linear progression where each transaction block has a child-parent relationship with either the preceding or succeeding block. For example, transaction block 10 has a child relationship with block 9 (preceding block) and a parent relationship with block 11 (succeeding block).

4. Anonymity

Blockchains operate on the principle of party identity abstraction which involves security by obscurity. What this means is that the identity of individual participants in the blockchain is not revealed. The only identifying information available on the blockchain is the blockchain address of participants. In order to carry out transactions, cryptographic keys are used to decrypt and encrypt the transaction inputs and outputs respectively.

Structure of a Blockchain

Blockchains depart from the data structure used in traditional computing, which is the database. A simple definition of a database is the way in which data is stored in a network. This data storage must obey some form of logic for it to be meaningful and useful to the participants of the network. The typical data storage structures used in traditional computing are rows, columns, CSV (comma separated values) etc.

Early on in the development of blockchain technology, it was apparent that the traditional database construct was not able to provide a robust framework for the blockchain, so another type of database was created specifically for the Bitcoin Blockchain (which was the first blockchain). All other blockchain iterations that have followed the Bitcoin Blockchain have kept this basic structure with slight modifications being made to suit the specific needs of the blockchain.

The structure of a blockchain is a back-linked list of transaction blocks that go all the way down to the Genesis block. An important part of this description is the **"back-linked"** aspect and what this means is that each block apart from the Genesis block takes its reference point from the preceding block in the chain. In other words, each block must have a parent relationship with a preceding block on the chain. When a new transaction block has been verified it is added to the blockchain stack by placing it on top of the preceding block. So you can imagine the blockchain to be a vertical stack of transaction blocks, like a geological formation with lots and lots of layers. It is the imagined vertical stacking of transaction blocks that give rise to terms like tip/top and block height.

Tip/Top:

This refers to the newly added transaction block to the blockchain. Because the blockchain is envisioned as a vertical stack, this newly added block is generally seen as the tip or top of the blockchain.

Block Height:

The block height of a transaction block on the blockchain is simply the distance between the block in question and the Genesis block. This distance is expressed in terms of the number of blocks starting from the Genesis block to the block in question. Again, because the blockchain is envisioned as a vertical stack of transaction blocks, this terminology is appropriate.

Parent-Child Relationship

As stated earlier, every block in the blockchain has either a Parent relationship or Child relationship with a block preceding or following it. As a rule, each block has only one parent block. Multiple blocks can have the same parent block when there are identical transactions existing on the blockchain at an instance of time. This appearance of multiple child blocks occurs when different nodes are independently verifying the same transaction at the same time. Most times, these multiple child scenarios only last for a short period of time as the blockchain will error-correct itself by choosing only one child block which then becomes the validated transaction block that is added to the blockchain.

Structure of a Block

If you liken the blockchain to an infinitely large book, then each transaction block can be thought of to be a page within the book. Once a transaction is verified, it becomes a page (block) of the blockchain (book). Continuing with this analogy, consider a page from a regular book, it has a header, footer, and in between, space for recording data. The same applies to the anatomy of a transaction block as it has a header, footer, and a space for recording data; in this case, the details of the transaction.

The header:

The header of a block contains a cryptographic hash of the parent block that precedes it. This cryptographic hash is the identifying marker that connects it with the parent block. The cryptographic hash is in most cases created with a SHA256 cryptographic hash algorithm. The chain which links the transaction blocks together is basically the hashes in the headers of each block.

The Footer:

In a page, the footer contains the page number and in the case of a transaction block, the footer section contains a specific description of the database. In computing terminology, this description is known as metadata. The metadata of a block is like a fingerprint that is specific to each block and to the details of the transactions in the block.

The Main Body:

This contains the validated list of digital assets and instruction statements that are involved in the transaction. All of this information is encrypted and includes the blockchain addresses of the participants, details of the transaction being made, amount of "coins" being transferred as well as some miscellaneous information that is specific to the transaction. In blockchains that have mining features, the main body of the block will also contain information relevant to the miner incentive reward i.e. the number of coins to be earned by the miner that successfully mines the block.

Chapter 3
Joining a Blockchain

In the natural progression of anyone who takes up an interest is Blockchain technology, once they have gained a fair bit of insight into the technology, the next logical step to take is to join a blockchain. Joining a blockchain is just one aspect of being part of the global digital currency industry which is fast becoming one of the largest industries in the world. As blockchains and cryptocurrencies become more popular and their acceptance begins to spread into diverse aspects of human life, the advantages of being part of the digital currency industry become even more profound. Since this book is dedicated to catering primarily for beginners in the world of blockchain technology, our focus will be restricted to joining a blockchain in a non-technical capacity i.e. nothing that has to do with coding or blockchain technology development.

Functions of Nodes in the Blockchain

Joining a blockchain simply means becoming a connected node in the blockchain network and contributing computing power to the maintenance of the network. Depending on the scalability of the blockchain network, becoming a node can be achieved using a computer or even a smartphone. There are different types of nodes in a blockchain which carry out specific functions that all add up to the proper functioning of the blockchain. In terms of functions, there are 4 basic node functions that are carried out by different nodes in a blockchain and they are:

1. Database function

   Nodes that carry out the database function have the full copy of the distributed ledger right up to the genesis block. These nodes are responsible for maintaining an up-to-date copy of the blockchain ledger.

2. Wallet

   There are nodes that are dedicated to the secure storage of the native digital tokens of a particular blockchain network. These nodes perform the wallet function. A wallet is anything that can securely store cryptocurrency tokens by means of a private key. Nodes carrying out the wallet function usually make use of a number of software implementations to enable them to function effectively.

3. Mining

   Using complex mathematical algorithms, some nodes participate in the validation of transactions which in some cases also leads to the creation of new cryptocurrency tokens. These nodes are performing the mining function.

4. Network Routing

   This is the most basic node function in the blockchain network. All nodes in a blockchain perform this function and it is essentially made of up two parts. The first part has to do with carrying out transactions which are the bread and butter of any blockchain. The second part of the network routing function involves the discovery and maintenance of P2P connections. All nodes can essentially act as a neighboring peer for a new node to connect to when joining the blockchain.

Types of Nodes

There are two types of nodes in the blockchain network and they are the Full Node and the SPV Node.

Full Nodes:

A full node is a term used to describe a node that maintains the full copy of the distributed ledger of transactions in the blockchain, all the way up to the genesis block. When a validated transaction is added to the local copy of a full node, it is then duplicated and broadcasted to the entire network. Once a consensus is reached that the newly validated transaction is a legitimate transaction, network-wide updates are sent so that the blockchain updates itself to reflect the newly added transaction block.

Based on the scalability of the blockchain in question, full nodes require a considerable amount of computer storage space to accommodate the data size of the blockchain. Full nodes have the ability to carry out their core functions without relying on peer connections for secondary support. They can also carry out each of the 4 aforementioned functions in a blockchain.

SPV Nodes:

SPV stands for Simplified Payment Verification and these types of nodes are useful for participants who do not want to run the full blockchain client on their computing devices. Sometimes it can be that these participants are making use of storage-constrained devices like tablets and smartphones and as such, they cannot run the full blockchain.

SPV, unlike full nodes, are specialty nodes meaning that they perform some, not all of the functions. In some instances, even when they can perform a blockchain function, they are not always able to do it independently as they will require a secondary support framework from a neighboring peer (e.g. verifying transactions). The reason for this is simple; SPV nodes do not have the full blockchain and as such, do not have all the information necessary to independently verify transactions.

The Extended Blockchain Network

Due to the ability of blockchains to allow the creation of programmable protocols to be built directly on top of their core functions, it is quite common to see a blockchain grow into something experts like to call the "Extended Blockchain". The extended blockchain goes beyond the full blockchain in that it contains all the specialized protocols that have been embedded into the core blockchain network.

Components of the Extended Blockchain Network

There are 3 broad components of the extended blockchain network and they are:

- The Core P2P Network

  This is the main blockchain network made up of interconnected nodes running the legacy blockchain client. This means the nodes are all running the default blockchain software. In the case of Bitcoin, the default software is called Bitcoin Core.

- Specialized Protocols

  These are specially programmed protocols that form part of the extended blockchain network. The nodes running these protocols do not necessarily use the legacy blockchain client. Most run derivative implementations of the legacy blockchain client.

- Miscellaneous Applications

  These are essentially network edge routing applications that are inserted into a blockchain to carry out payment processing services and other financial transactions. The nodes running these applications tend to use derivatives of the legacy blockchain client but without the need for wallet or mining functions.

The Blockchain Network Discovery Process for New Nodes

The following is a highly generalized process by which new nodes can discover and connect to a blockchain network. Each blockchain has some specific parameters but the general principle remains the same. Joining a blockchain network involves establishing a connection with the P2P network of that blockchain.

It is important to point out that deciding to join a blockchain network means that you are making a conscious decision to be a part of the servicing and maintenance of the network. The generalized process involved in the discovery and connection to a blockchain network are as follows:

1. Download and install the blockchain client onto your computer, tablet or smartphone. Depending on the data storage capacity and the scalability of the blockchain you are connecting to, you may decide to download the full client or an abridged version.

2. Initiate the blockchain client on your device and perform a simple DNS query. This provides a list of IP addresses of stable neighboring nodes that you can connect to.

3. The next step is to connect to a neighboring node by means of a "handshake"; a computer term that represents the formation of a connection between two node points by means of command prompts.

4. The neighboring node acknowledges the handshake, and a connection is established between the two nodes. The new node now has one point of access into the blockchain but for stability, multiple access paths into the blockchain network are required. The reason for this is due to the fact that nodes can become disconnected over time and if all the access paths into the blockchain become disconnected, a node will lose connectivity to the blockchain and will have to begin the connection process all over again.

5. Some blockchains have protocols that automate the formation of new connections after the first connection has been made. IP addresses of multiple neighboring nodes are sent to the new node to connect to. It is important to remember that the more nodes you connect to, the more computing power you will spend while running the blockchain.

Once these steps have been successfully completed, you are now a participant in a blockchain network. Many blockchains have a dormancy detection protocol as part of the operating architecture. This dormancy detection works by checking the status of each node periodically and if, after a set period of time, there is no activity detected from a node; it is deemed to have become inactive and is disconnected from the blockchain.

Chapter 4
Understanding Blockchain Transactions

The essence of a blockchain is to create a secure environment for network participants to safely carry out transactions. These transactions are then recorded within the distributed ledger which is shared to all participants of the network. The entire blockchain architecture exists to make sure that transactions once verified, cannot be altered in any way. This singular ledger that records all the transactions in a network has the potential for a wide range of applications.

What is a Transaction?

A lot of mention has been made of the word "transaction" in this book. If one were to go online as well, there are also tons of references being made to this same word whenever blockchain technology is being discussed. In actual fact, a transaction is a common enough term in digital technology and it always has to do with some form of data exchange. For example, when trying to read an article on a Wikipedia, the user attempts to connect to the Wikipedia link. In actual fact, the user's computer being the client is trying to establish a connection with the Wikipedia server in order to gain access to that article. When the connection is successfully made, the information appears on a screen and a transaction is said to have taken place. This is a digital transaction at its most basic level. With this sort of understanding in mind, the reader can begin to appreciate just how diverse digital transactions can be once viewed in the context of data exchange between at least two nodes.

In blockchain technology, a transaction is a database on which the encrypted digital asset transfer (or group of assets transfer) is recorded upon. In a blockchain, participants are regularly transferring digital assets and these digital assets could potentially be anything from cryptocurrencies like bitcoins, to contract milestones etc. Such is the power of the blockchain that Individuals, Organizations, and even Governments now have the ability to introduce trustless authentication and verification for a host of transactions. The fact that these transactions are encrypted, provides a level of security that is unmatched by anything that exists today.

Blockchain Transaction Lifecycle

There is a process that every transaction must undergo from when it is initiated to when it is validated and becomes a part of the blockchain. This process is described by the blockchain transaction lifecycle. In each of the known blockchains available today, there are many subtle differences in this process. In this section, a simplified approximation of the process will be presented to enable the reader get a fair idea of the steps involved in the process.

For the purpose of this description, a transaction will be carried out on a hypothetical blockchain using a hypothetical cryptocurrency called Satocoin. The transaction is being carried out by a girl named Lulu who wants to buy a sweater from an online store. Remember that a cryptocurrency is the native digital currency of a blockchain or blockchain-based application.

While browsing for sweaters online, Lulu comes across a sweater she likes and clicks the "buy now" button which takes her to the payment page. She chooses Satocoin as her payment option and she inputs her public key to initiate the payment. Now the Satocoin blockchain network must verify that she has enough Satocoin in her wallet to afford the sweater, which by the way, costs 20 Satocoin.

The stages this transaction will pass through are as follows:

- Initiation:

  Once Lulu clicks the "buy now" button and proceeds to enter in her wallet information, the transaction is said to have been initiated. Lulu signs this transaction using her public-private key combination. She does this by entering her public key during the payment process. This initiated transaction that has been signed is now ready for broadcast and propagation.

- Pre-Validation Broadcast & Propagation:

  Nodes within the network discover Lulu's transaction and carry out checks to ascertain its validity. These checks involve examining the data structure within the transaction and once it is deemed valid it is propagated to the entire network. By a process called *"flooding"*, this propagated transaction becomes accessible to more nodes within the network. This process is a rapid, ensuring that in a few seconds, every node in the network has received the new transaction.

- Validation:

As more nodes receive the transaction, its validation becomes more established. As each node validates the transaction, it propagates it further within the network. This ensures that an invalid transaction doesn't become deeply propagated within the network, wasting computing power in the process.

Once the transaction has been validated, it sits in the transaction pool (memory pool) where it waits to be grouped with other transactions into a block on its way to the verification process (mining).

The Blockchain Transaction Verification Process

This process describes the means by which a validated transaction is verified, in order for it to become a part of the blockchain ledger. In many blockchains applications, this process is referred to as *"mining"*. It is the termination of the transaction lifecycle during which the transaction becomes recorded in a block on the blockchain. It is important to note that not all blockchains have a mining process but for the purpose of this section, the focus will be limited to blockchains in which the verification of transactions is via a block mining process.

What is Blockchain Mining?

Mining is another of those terms that one hears repeatedly in the blockchain space. The literal understanding of the word itself applies to a part of what the process achieves, in that it leads to the creation ("mining") of new coins in the blockchain. A coin is the generic term used to describe a cryptocurrency.

In a blockchain network, mining refers to the process by which a transaction block is verified and added as a block on the blockchain. This process also leads to the creation of new coins which are given as a reward to the node that successfully "mines" the block. In some blockchains, there is no reward for mining the block as the mining receives a transaction fee. In any case, there is always some form of reward (or incentive) for mining nodes in a blockchain network.

Most mining processes are based on cryptographic hashing, where mathematical computations are used to solve the complex mathematical algorithms that make up the block header parameters. Recall, that block headers contain a cryptographic hash. Imagine this hash to be like a complex math problem requiring a solution. It is the job of the mining node to discover the unique solution to this problem in order to verify the block. The blockchain is coded in a way that makes this solution difficult to obtain yet easy to verify by other nodes.

Blockchain mining helps to maintain the structural integrity of the blockchain. With so many nodes working independently, it can be difficult to ensure uniformity of process but mining solves this process easily by introducing mathematical proofs which are a universal language.

Steps involved in Verifying a Blockchain Transaction

Remember Lulu's transaction? Having been validated, it now sits in something called the memory pool where it will await the authentication of a mining node. The memory pool (or transaction pool) is a place in the blockchain environment where all the validated transactions temporarily reside while waiting for authentication by mining nodes during the mining process.

The verification process for transactions in a blockchain is also a step-wise process. Different blockchains utilize diverse mathematical proofs but the focus will be given to the proof-of-work algorithm in this section. This is the mining algorithm used by bitcoin. The steps are as follows.

- Identification

    Mining nodes search the memory pool, looking for unconfirmed transactions. One of them will come across Lulu's transaction, alongside a group of other unconfirmed transactions. These transactions are then aggregated into something called a *"candidate block"*. The candidate block is an aggregation of data structures (transactions) into a single block for mining.

- Computation

This is where the cryptographic hashing process takes place. Mining nodes will seek to find a solution for the proof-of-work algorithm of the candidate block that contains Lulu's transaction. This action is being carried out simultaneously by numerous mining nodes on the blockchain. All of them race against each other to arrive at the solution first so that they can claim the reward.

The basic principle in the computation stage is to obtain a value that is less than that of a specific target. Part of the architecture of the blockchain specifies a target that is unique for every candidate block. During the mining process, a mining node has to arrive at a value that is less than this specific target. Only then can the block be said to have been mined. Think of this specific target to be a picture puzzle. Only by fitting the pieces together can the puzzle be completed.

Using hashing techniques, mining nodes will perform multiple trial and error computations using something called *"nonce values"* until a solution for the proof-of-work algorithm is obtained. The common hash function used by most blockchains that favor the proof-of-work algorithm is the SHA256 hashing function.

During the trial and error hashing process, when a nonce value does not produce a value that is less than that of the specific target value, it is modified. After modification, the process is repeated until the block header value of the candidate block becomes less than that of the specific target. Depending on the computing power of the mining hardware being utilized, as many as 1 quadrillion trial and error attempts might be required before the correct nonce value is arrived at. For this reason, a considerable amount of computing power and electricity is utilized by large mining node setups.

- Broadcast

A mining node will eventually be successful in finding the solution to the proof-of-work algorithm for the candidate block that contains Lulu's transaction. Once this happens, the mining node will broadcast it to the entire network for others to verify. The verification process involves examining the proof-of-work solution to make sure that it is indeed of a lower value than that of the target. There are also some other checks that are carried out to ascertain the validity of the solution.

The way blockchains are built, the mining process is a complex one but the process of verifying the work done by miners is actually simple and straightforward. The complexity of the mining operation adds a robust fidelity component to the network while the ease of verifying drastically speeds up transaction lag times. This is one of the many ingenious aspects of blockchain technology that makes it such a revolutionary concept.

- Majority Consensus

At this stage, the mined candidate block containing Lulu's transaction is being broadcast throughout the entire network. Other nodes review the solution to see if it is correct. With each successful validation by peer nodes, a distributed consensus begins to develop as these peer nodes add the mined candidate block to their local copy of the blockchain. Soon, this distributed consensus becomes a majority consensus and the candidate block becomes a legitimate block on the blockchain.

- Addition

Once the majority consensus is formed, the mined candidate block becomes a verified block and it will now reside permanently on the blockchain. At any time, participants in the network can examine the block and they will find Lulu's 20 Satocoin payment. The successful mining node also receives a reward for being able to mine the block.

Chapter 5
Understanding Blockchain Consensus

On the surface of it, the premise of the blockchain technology framework with its decentralized control seems elegant. The removal of a central server has a lot of benefits that have been explored to some degree in the preceding chapters of this book. Say what you will about the current mainstream setup of computer networks, the presence of a central authority that validates, authorizes and authenticates represents a defined structure in terms of how the system operates. In a blockchain, there is no hierarchy, and as such, everyone can do what they like, or can they?

One of the major issues that delayed the successful implementation of a digital currency framework long before Bitcoin was the problem of *"double-spending"*. Digital currencies are just tokens issued by a network that participants can spend in carrying out transactions. How can a network guard against people spending the same token that has been spent in a previous transaction? This problem of double spending seemed almost impossible to solve until the Satoshi Nakamoto introduced the blockchain as part of the Bitcoin white paper.

There were a lot of revolutionary aspects to the bitcoin white paper, especially with the elegant way in which the blockchain was used to successfully implement the DLT framework that many have been trying to do for decades. The use of a carefully constructed majority consensus protocol is what enables the DLT to maintain singularity which is required for the optimal functioning of the network. The meaning of this is quite simple – there is only one ledger which records all the transactions on the blockchain and on this blockchain, there are numerous nodes working independently of each other. How then do you make sure that they all hold the same information? This issue was addressed by means of majority consensus protocol.

What is a Consensus?

Simply put, a consensus refers to an agreement between the participants of the network. This agreement can be anything from transaction validation to the implementation of new protocols that will change the way the network operates. In a decentralized network, there is a form of democracy at play and that means that changes cannot be forced upon the participants. A great majority of the nodes have to agree or else, the system will become deadlocked. In the absence of consensus, a blockchain will not achieve network unity and the resultant division leads to the formation of failures within the system. If left unresolved, the system collapses and *"hard forks"* emerge.

Formation of the Majority Consensus

Within the normal functioning of the blockchain, there are always bound to be times when there is a lack of agreement between participating nodes on what the blockchain should look like. These temporary disagreements are usually resolved once a majority consensus is achieved. In the following narrative, a brief look at how the formation of the majority consensus solves these temporary disagreements will be examined.

In order to completely understand this narrative, a few facts must be made known to the reader.

1. There are numerous mining nodes in a blockchain network.

2. More than one mining node can create the same candidate block, mine it and broadcast it to the network at roughly the same time.

3. These different versions of the same candidate block can be verified by different nodes creating a situation where there is now more than one version of the blockchain in existence.

Blockchain Classification

For a blockchain to function properly, the ledger must be uniform. What then happens when the ledger isn't uniform is quite simple, a majority consensus is formed. It is true that there is only one true blockchain that contains the accurate distributed ledger but for the purpose of ensuring a robust network, nodes maintain three different blockchains which are adjusted periodically. These chains are as follows:

- The Main Chain

  The main chain is made up of all the blocks connected to the true blockchain. It is usually the chain with the highest cumulative difficulty associated with the constituent blocks on the chain and in most cases, it is the longest chain.

- The Secondary Chain

  The secondary chain is made up of blocks that have branched off from the main chain. These blocks are *"siblings"* of blocks in the main chain, i.e. they share the same parent block with a block on the main chain. These blocks are valid in themselves but due to the competitive nature of the block mining process where multiple blocks mine and broadcast the same candidate block at the same time.

The blockchain will always error-correct itself and as such, nodes do not jettison their secondary chains as they could become the main chain in future. This phenomenon will be explored fully in the blockchain fork section of this chapter.

- The Orphan Chain

The orphan chain is made up of blocks that do not have any parent block in the main chain or in the secondary chain. As stated earlier in this book, every block with the exception of the genesis block must have a relationship (child-parent relationship) with a preexisting block. The information in the header of every block in the main chain and secondary chain references some previously verified block on the blockchain.

So how do these orphan blocks come about? Sometimes, a full node will come across a mined block that has no child relationship with any preexisting block on the blockchain. The full node will examine the block and find that it is indeed valid but there is no information concerning where it should be placed on the blockchain. One constant reason for this is due to the fact that the parent block in question hasn't been fully propagated within the network. Remember that many mining operations are being carried out per second and sometimes, there is a slight delay in getting the full blockchain to be on the same page.

What happens is that the full node will place this orphan block in the orphan pool. When the parent block becomes fully propagated, this orphan block will be added to the blockchain. For blockchains that have mining activities as part of their operating protocol, mined blocks are timestamped two hours in the future to cover up for unavoidable time lags.

The Longest Chain Rule

No, this isn't a something out of a Chemistry textbook. The longest chain rule is the means by which a majority consensus is achieved when disagreements arise in the blockchain network with regard to what the current blockchain should be. System-wide harmony is required for a blockchain to function otherwise the system will begin to develop faults and failures will start to creep in. Having multiple nodes working independently without any central means of organization requires a standardized method of achieving unity.

The longest chain rule states that when there is a disagreement as to what constitutes the main chain and the secondary chain, the resolution lies in the fact that the main chain is the one with the highest cumulative difficulty associated with its constituent blocks. This chain with the highest cumulative difficulty is also the longest chain, hence the term. It is for this reason that nodes always maintain the secondary chain because as new mined blocks are discovered and ready to be added to the blockchain, the secondary chain can become the main chain, and vice-versa.

By having such a simple, yet elegant means of settling such a dispute that it is an integral part of the functioning of blockchains, maintaining system-wide harmony becomes far easier. This process is automatic; once the secondary chain becomes the primary chain, the changes are adopted instantaneously and the blockchain proceeds.

Blockchain Forks

No introduction into blockchain technology will be complete without looking at blockchain forks. In this last section of the book, the focus will now be shifted to providing a brief summary of what forks are, how they occur and how they are resolved.

Definition

A fork is the emergence of two potential paths forward in the blockchain network. These potential paths forward can refer to either the structure of the blockchain or the implementation of new protocols that govern the network. The structure of the blockchain here refers to what should be the true chain and what should be the secondary chain. Implementation of new protocols has to with changes that affect parameters like scalability, mining algorithm and a host of other blockchain governing parameters. The focus of this book will be limited to forks that have to do with the blockchain structure.

How They Occur

To explain how forks occur, let us revisit Lulu's 20 Satocoin transaction that has already been mined as part of a candidate block. Let us assume that prior to that transaction, there were 49 blocks on the blockchain. The candidate block containing Lulu's transaction should become the 50th block once it is added to the blockchain.

It is quite possible that two different mining nodes mined the candidate block that contains Lulu's transaction and broadcast it to the network at roughly the same time. Let's call these competing mining nodes X and Y and their corresponding blocks 50X and 50Y. Mining node X will broadcast block 50X to its neighboring peers who will then add it to the local copy of their blockchains and propagate it further. The same thing will happen with the neighboring nodes of mining node Y. At this point in the network, there are two distinct true chains, one with 50X and another with 50Y. Both of them have the same parent block.

Soon, nodes that have 50X on their blockchain will come across block 50Y and notice that it is a sibling of 50X in that it shares the same parent block as 50X. These nodes will automatically add block 50Y to their secondary chain. The same thing also happens with nodes that have 50Y on their main chain. Soon, they will discover 50X and see that it is a sibling block to the 50Y they have on their main chain. They will then add 50X to their secondary chain.

At this point, a fork has occurred in the blockchain and it needs to be resolved.

How they are Resolved

Forks of this nature are resolved by adopting the chain with the longest cumulative difficulty (the longest chain rule). Continuing with the scenario that has been set up from the previous section, some miners will be mining based on the blockchain that ends with 50X while others will be mining based on 50Y.

Let us assume that a miner working with 50X wins the hashing race and mines block 51. This block 51 will be a child of 50X but will have no relationship whatsoever with block 50Y. Block 52 will be broadcast within the network and nodes having 50X on their main chain will be able to add it to their main chain.

However, nodes having block 50Y on their main chain will find that block 51 has no relationship with 50Y so they will check to see if it has a relationship with block 50X on their secondary chain. When they discover that 51 is a child of block 50X on their secondary chain, they will realize that their secondary chains have become longer than their primary chains. They will check the cumulative difficulties of both and see that their secondary chain is indeed higher than their primary chain. What happens next is that these nodes will reconverge and their secondary chains become their main chains and vice-versa.

They will then broadcast this change to the network and soon, the blockchain will error-correct itself across the entire network. In this way, the fork is resolved after only one block. In fact, it is theoretically impossible for this type of fork to extend beyond one block.

Conclusion

Thank you for purchasing this book and taking the time to read its contents thoroughly. A lot of effort has been put into making sure the language of the book is clear and concise so that readers can easily understand the more technical aspects of the subject matter.

By completing the beginners' guide, you should now have a good understanding of Blockchain Technology in terms of all the basic elements that come together to provide the framework for blockchains to function. It is hoped that all the information contained within this book has added value to you, the reader.

If you have enjoyed reading this book, I would crave your indulgence in leaving a review on Amazon. I absolutely welcome your honest feedback about the book in general and any specific comments you may have.

If you enjoyed this book as much as I've enjoyed writing it, you can subscribe* to my email list for exclusive content and sneak peaks of my future books.

Click the link below:
http://eepurl.com/du_qcj

OR

Use the QR Code:

(*Must be 13 years or older to subscribe)

Conclusion

Made in the USA
Las Vegas, NV
10 February 2021

17552351R00035